# Harris

**by Iain Gray**

LangSyne

PUBLISHING

WRITING *to* REMEMBER

79 Main Street, Newtongrange,
Midlothian EH22 4NA
Tel: 0131 344 0414
E-mail: info@lang-syne.co.uk
www.langsyneshop.co.uk

Design by Dorothy Meikle
Printed by Printwell Ltd
© Lang Syne Publishers Ltd 2022



ISBN 978-1-85217-660-0

# Harris

**MOTTO:**

Everywhere to remember one's country.

**CREST:**

A golden hedgehog.

**NAME** variations include:
Hariss
Harrie
Harries
Harrison
Harry

*Chapter one:*

# Origins of Welsh surnames

by Iain Gray

***If you don't know where you came from, you won't know where you're going* is a frequently quoted observation and one that has a particular resonance today when there has been a marked upsurge in interest in genealogy, with increasing numbers of people curious to trace their family roots.**

Main sources for genealogical research include census returns and official records of births, marriages and deaths – and the key to unlocking the detail they contain is obviously a family surname, one that has been 'inherited' and passed from generation to generation.

No matter our station in life, we all have a surname – but it was not until about the middle of the fourteenth century that the practice of being identified by a particular, or 'fixed', surname became commonly established throughout the British Isles.

Previous to this, it was normal for a person to be identified through the use of only a forename.

Wales, however, known in the Welsh language as *Cymru*, is uniquely different – with the use of what are known as patronymic names continuing well into the fifteenth century and, in remote rural areas, up until the early nineteenth century.

Patronymic names are ones where a son takes his father's forename, or Christian name, as his surname.

Examples of patronymic names throughout the British Isles include 'Johnson', indicating 'son of John', while specifically in Scotland 'son of' was denoted by the prefix Mc or Mac – with 'MacDonald', for example, meaning 'son of Donald.'

Early Welsh law, known as *Cyfraith Hywel*, *The Law of Hywel*, introduced by Hywel the Good, who ruled from Prestatyn to Pembroke between 915 AD and 950 AD, stipulated that a person's name should indicate their ancestry – the name in effect being a type of 'family tree.'

This required the prefixes *ap* or *ab* – derived from *mab*, meaning 'son of' being placed before the person's baptismal name.

In the case of females, the suffixes *verch* or *ferch*, sometimes shortened to *vch* or *vz* would be attached to their Christian name to indicate 'daughter of.'

In some cases, rather than being known for

example as *Llewellyn ap Thomas – Llewellyn son of Thomas* – Llewellyn's name would incorporate an 'ancestral tree' going back much earlier than his father.

One source gives the example of *Llewellyn ap Thomas ap Dafydd ap Evan ap Owen ap John* – meaning *Llewellyn son of Thomas son of Dafydd son of Evan son of Owen son of John.*

This leads to great confusion, to say the least, when trying to trace a person's ancestry back to a particular family – with many people having the forenames, for example, of Llewellyn, Thomas, Owen or John.

The first Act of Union between Wales and England that took place in 1536 during the reign of Henry VIII required that all Welsh names be registered in an Anglicised form – with *Hywel*, for example, becoming Howell, or Powell, and *Gruffydd* becoming Griffiths.

An early historical example of this concerns William ap John Thomas, standard bearer to Henry VIII, who became William Jones.

In many cases – as in Davies and Williams – an s was simply added to the original patronymic name, while in other cases the prefix *ap* or *ab* was contracted to *p* or *b* to prefix the name – as in *ab Evan* to form Bevan and *ap Richard* to form Pritchard.

Other original Welsh surnames – such as Morgan, originally *Morcant* – derive from ancient Celtic sources, while others stem from a person's physical characteristics – as in *Gwyn* or *Wynne* a nickname for someone with fair hair, *Gough* or *Gooch* denoting someone with red hair or a ruddy complexion, *Gethin* indicating swarthy or ugly and *Lloyd* someone with brown or grey hair.

With many popular surnames found today in Wales being based on popular Christian names such as John, this means that what is known as the 'stock' or 'pool' of names is comparatively small compared to that of common surnames found in England, Scotland and Ireland.

This explains why, in a typical Welsh village or town with many bearers of a particular name not necessarily being related, they were differentiated by being known, for example, as 'Jones the butcher', 'Jones the teacher' and 'Jones the grocer.'

Another common practice, dating from about the nineteenth century, was to differentiate among families of the same name by prefixing it with the mother's surname or hyphenating the name.

The history of the origins and development of Welsh surnames is inextricably bound up with the nation's frequently turbulent history and its rich culture.

Speaking a Celtic language known as Brythonic, which would gradually evolve into Welsh, the natives were subjected to Roman invasion in 48 AD, and in the following centuries to invasion by the Anglo-Saxons, Vikings and Normans.

Under England's ruthless and ambitious Edward I, the nation was fortified with castles between 1276 and 1295 to keep the 'rebellious' natives in check – but this did not prevent a series of bloody uprisings against English rule that included, most notably, Owain Glyndŵr's rebellion in 1400.

Politically united with England through the first Act of Union in 1536, becoming part of the Kingdom of Great Britain in 1707 and part of the United Kingdom in 1801, it was in 1999 that *Cynulliad Cenedlaethol Cymru*, the National Assembly for Wales, was officially opened by the Queen.

Welsh language and literature has flourished throughout the nation's long history.

In what is known as the Heroic Age, early Welsh poets include the late sixth century Taliesin and Aneirin, author of *Y Gododdin*.

Discovered in a thirteenth century manuscript but thought to date from anywhere between the seventh and eleventh centuries, it refers to the kingdom of Gododdin that took in south-east Scotland and

Northumberland and was part of what was once the Welsh territory known as *Hen Ogledd, The Old North.*

Commemorating Gododdin warriors who were killed in battle against the Angles of Bernicia and Deira at Catraith in about 600 AD, the manuscript – known as *Llyfr Aneirin, Book of Aneirin* – is now in the precious care of Cardiff City Library.

Other important early works by Welsh poets include the fourteenth century *Red Book of Hergest*, now held in the Bodleian Library, Oxford, and the *White Book of Rhydderch*, kept in the National Library of Wales, Aberystwyth.

William Morgan's translation of the Bible into Welsh in 1588 is hailed as having played an important role in the advancement of the Welsh language, while in I885 Dan Isaac Davies founded the first Welsh language society.

It was in 1856 that Evan James and his son James James composed the rousing Welsh national anthem *Hen Wlad Fynhadad – Land of My Fathers*, while in the twentieth century the poet Dylan Thomas gained international fame and acclaim with poems such as *Under Milk Wood*.

The nation's proud cultural heritage is also celebrated through *Eisteddfod Genedlaethol Cymru*, the National Eisteddfod of Wales, the annual festival of music, literature and performance that is held across the nation and which traces its roots back to 1176 when Rhys ap Gruffyd, who ruled the territory of Deheubarth from 1155 to 1197, hosted a magnificent festival of poetry and song at his court in Cardigan.

The 2011 census for Wales unfortunately shows that the number of people able to speak the language has declined from 20.8% of the population of just under 3.1 million in 2001 to 19% – but overall the nation's proud culture, reflected in its surnames, still flourishes.

Many Welsh families proudly boast the heraldic device known as a Coat of Arms, as featured on our front cover.

The central motif of the Coat of Arms would originally have been what was borne on the shield of a warrior to distinguish himself from others on the battlefield.

Not featured on the Coat of Arms, but highlighted on page three, is the family motto and related crest – with the latter frequently different from the central motif.

Echoes of a far distant past can still be found in our surnames and they can be borne with pride in commemoration of our forebears.

*Chapter two:*

# Turbulent times

**Derived from the popular forename 'Harry', in turn a pet form of 'Henry', 'Harris' is a patronymic surname indicating 'son of Harry' – while 'Henry', of Germanic roots, denotes 'head, or chief, of the house.'**

It was in the wake of the Norman Conquest of 1066 that the surname, in common with many others, became popularised throughout the British Isles.

A key date in not only English but also Welsh history, by 1066 England had become a nation with several powerful competitors to the throne.

In what were extremely complex family, political and military machinations, the monarch was Harold II, who had succeeded to the throne following the death of Edward the Confessor.

But his right was contested by two powerful competitors – his brother-in-law King Harold Hardrada of Norway, in alliance with Tostig, Harold II's brother, and Duke William II of Normandy.

On October 14, Harold II encountered a mighty invasion force led by William that had landed at Hastings, in East Sussex.

Harold drew up a strong defensive position, at the top of Senlac Hill, building a shield wall to repel William's cavalry and infantry.

The Normans suffered heavy losses, but through a combination of the deadly skill of their archers and the ferocious determination of their cavalry they eventually won the day.

Anglo-Saxon morale had collapsed on the battlefield as word spread through the ranks that Harold, the last of the Anglo-Saxon kings, had been killed.

William was declared King of England on December 25, and the complete subjugation of his Anglo-Saxon subjects followed, with those Normans who had fought on his behalf rewarded with lands – a pattern later repeated in Wales.

Invading across the Welsh Marches, the borderland between England and Wales, the Normans gradually consolidated gains by building castles – but under a succession of Welsh leaders resistance proved strong.

But it was brutally crushed in 1283 under England's ruthless and ambitious Edward I, who ordered the building or repair of at least 17 castles and in 1302 proclaiming his son and heir, the future Edward II, as Prince of Wales, a title known in Welsh as *Tywysog Cymru*.

It is in Pembrokeshire, one of what are known as the thirteen historic Welsh counties, that the Harris name is particularly identified.

This means that from earliest times the ancestors of those who would come to bear the name were at the centre of the high drama that is the nation's frequently turbulent history.

Known in the Welsh language as 'Sir Benfro', with 'Sir' indicating 'County', modern-day Pembrokeshire, in the southwest of Wales, has Haverfordwest as its county town, while previously it was Pembroke.

It is a rather unique county, in that in 1138, during the reign of England's King Stephen, it became divided between a predominantly Welsh speaking north and a mainly English speaking south.

So noticeable is this divide that the linguistic 'border' even has its own designation, known as the *Landsker Line* – derived from an old Anglo-Saxon term – while the south of the county is known as 'Little England in Wales.'

Three eighteenth century Welsh brothers of the Harris name stamped their mark on the historical record through wholly separate endeavours and pursuits.

The sons of a carpenter originally from Llangadock, Carmarthenshire and who later settled at Trefeca – then spelled 'Trefecka' – about a mile south of

Talgarth, Breconshire, they were the leading religious reformer Howell Harris, the astronomer, navigator and King's Assay Master at the Royal Mint Joseph Harris and the wealthy tailor and merchant Thomas Harris.

Known as 'The Apostle of Wales', Howell Harris, whose first name also appears in some accounts as 'Howel', was born in Trefeca in 1714.

An adherent of the form of religious evangelism known as Methodism – particularly popular throughout Wales – he was employed as a schoolmaster from 1732 to 1735 and later, along with Daniel Rowland, Howel Davies and William Williams, formed an association that forged an alliance with the Methodist movement in England.

The alliance, however, was split by dissension over complex matters of doctrine and by 1750 Welsh Methodism had split into two sects – one led by Harris.

Two years later, he established a 'Family' in Trefeca from among his loyal supporters – a form of religious 'commune' with its members supporting themselves through the practice of a number of trades.

Also interested in agriculture, particularly the latest innovations in farming methods, Harris was one of the founders in 1755 of the Breconshire Agricultural Society, recognised as the first of its kind in Wales.

A charismatic preacher and composer of a number of hymns, he died in 1773, while his entry in the Dictionary of Welsh Biography states in glowing terms that "…his unceasing enthusiasm and his unbounded desire to save souls carried everything before him in the early days of the religious renaissance.

"The influence which he has had on the life of his people proves that he was the greatest spiritual force in his generation and many believe that he was the greatest Welshman of his age."

Following a much different path, his elder brother Joseph, born in 1702, was apprenticed for a time to a maternal uncle as a blacksmith.

Despite the gulf in their social standing, as a young man he became betrothed to Anne Jones, daughter of Thomas Jones, High Sheriff of Brecknock, and it was through his powerful connections that he gained introductions to important figures in the worlds of science and commerce.

Gaining employment with the South Sea Company, and while engaged in trading the company's goods in Vera Cruz, Mexico, he was able to indulge his passion and talent for astronomy and navigation by observing and describing a partial eclipse of the sun and establishing the latitude and longitude of Vera Cruz.

These observations, which had been sponsored

by the astronomer Edmond Halley, whom Harris had met in London, were later published in the *Transactions* of the scientific think-tank The Royal Society.

Back on British shores, Harris published the landmark *Treatise on Navigation*, followed later by other important works that include *Description and Use of the Globes*.

While still continuing with his astronomical and navigational observations and writings, he was in need of more secure paid employment and, with the help of influential friends, was appointed assistant to the King's Assay Master at the Royal Mint.

Promoted to King's Assay Master in 1749, he died in 1764.

His younger brother Thomas, born in 1705, was apprenticed as a tailor to an uncle in London when he was aged fourteen – later branching out on his own and accruing a fortune through securing lucrative army contracts for items of military apparel.

Returning to his native Wales after 40 years in London, the rather unconventional Thomas Harris – unmarried but fathering at least three children – was nevertheless appointed Sheriff of Brecknock; having bought the estates of Trefeca and Tregunter, he died in 1782.

*Chapter three:*

# Fame and infamy

**One particularly tragic bearer of the Harris name was the American socialite Clara Hamilton Harris who, along with her then fiancé Major Henry Rathbone, was a guest of President Abraham Lincoln and First Lady Mary Lincoln when the president was assassinated during a performance at Ford's Theatre, Washington, D.C., in April of 1865.**

Born in 1834 in Albany, New York, a daughter of New York Senator Ira Harris and his first wife Louisa, she was aged eleven when her mother died.

Three years later, her father married Pauline Rathbone, widow of a wealthy merchant and mayor of Albany and, rather unusually, it was with her stepbrother Henry Rathbone that Clara became engaged and later married.

The outbreak of the American Civil War in 1861 interrupted their marriage plans, with Rathbone rising to the rank of major in the Union Army.

It was following the end of the conflict that Clara and her fiancé accepted an invitation to join the president and his wife in the Presidential Box at Ford's

Theatre to watch a performance of the play *Our American Cousin*.

While they were enjoying the performance, John Wilkes Booth entered the box and shot the president in the back of the head.

Attempting to apprehend Booth as he fled the scene, Rathbone was viciously slashed from his shoulder to his left elbow with a Bowie knife.

Clara's white dress, face and hands were stained with his blood as she attempted to aid him.

Despite the severity of his wound, Rathbone accompanied his fiancé, the First Lady and others to a nearby house where doctors battled in vain to save the president's life.

Rathbone recovered from his physical injuries, but he remained mentally distraught for the rest of his life – blaming himself for not having prevented the president's assassination.

Clara and Major Rathbone eventually married in July of 1867 and, attempting to lay to rest their grim memories of the assassination, sought a new life in Germany.

But Rathbone became increasingly mentally unstable over the following years until finally, in December of 1883, he attacked his children in a fit of madness.

Trying to protect them, Clara was shot and killed by her husband – who then attempted to take his own life by stabbing himself five times.

Committed to a German mental asylum, the mentally tortured Rathbone died in 1911 – while he was buried next to the wife he had murdered 28 years earlier.

On a rather supernatural note, before leaving the United States for a new life in Germany, Clara had kept the blood-stained dress she had worn on the night of the assassination – unable to bring herself to either wash or destroy it.

Eventually storing it in a closet, she had had the closet bricked up after being convinced she had received an ethereal visitation from the president's ghost.

In the following century and during the dark days of the Second World War, Sir Arthur Harris, known as "Bomber" Harris and by some of his detractors as "Butcher" Harris, was the British Air Chief Marshall born in Cheltenham, Gloucestershire, in 1892.

It was as Air Officer Commanding-in-Chief of RAF Bomber Command during the Second World War that, from early in 1943, he was in charge of the devastating and controversial 'area', as opposed to 'precision' bombing of German cities such as Dresden – a policy with which he had been tasked by his political masters.

Raised to the peerage as a Baronet in 1953 at the insistence of Winston Churchill, after having earlier refused the honour, he died in 1984.

The controversy over his bombing strategy continues to this day – with the late Queen Mother being jeered by protestors when she unveiled a statue of Harris outside the RAF Church of St Clement Danes, London, in 1992.

One infamous bearer of the otherwise proud name of Harris was Eric Harris, the American high school student who, on April 20, 1999, along with his friend and fellow student Dylan Klebold, shot and killed thirteen people and injured 24 others in what became known as the Columbine High School Massacre.

Born in 1981 in Wichita, Kansas, the son of a U.S. Air Force transport pilot, Harris was aged thirteen when his family settled in Littleton, Colorado, while Klebold was born in 1981 in Lakewood, Colorado.

Becoming friends after enrolling at Columbine High School, Columbine, the highly technically-literate pair were inseparable, with both producing video productions for the school and maintaining its computer server.

It was on the morning of April 20 that fellow student Brooks Brown, with whom Harris had already had a number of altercations, saw him arrive late for morning classes.

Brown mentioned his lateness to him – Harris normally being punctual to the point of obsession – and he replied with the enigmatic warning: "It doesn't matter anymore. Brooks, I like you now. Get out of here. Go home."

Sensing trouble, Brown immediately left the school premises and it was while walking away that he heard a fusillade of gunshots.

He alerted the police on a borrowed mobile 'phone – but a massacre was by now well under way.

Harris had arrived at school in his car, while Klebold had arrived a short time later, also by car.

Lugging two heavy gym bags each containing a 20-pound home-made propane bomb, they embarked on a lethal shooting spree after dumping the bombs in the cafeteria where they failed to explode.

Armed with an arsenal of weapons that included shotguns, a Hi-Point carbine and a semi-automatic TEC-DC9 handgun, in what is the deadliest attack ever carried out on an American high school, in the space of 20 minutes they killed twelve of their fellow students and a teacher and injured 24 others.

Ten of their victims were killed in the school

library, and it was from one of its windows that the pair opened fire on police who had sped to the scene.

Only a short time later, a teacher who had locked herself inside a break room along with a number of other staff and students, heard Harris and Klebold shout out in unison: "One! Two! Three!"

In an apparent suicide pact, Harris then fired a shotgun through the roof of his mouth, while Klebold shot himself through the left temple with the semi-automatic handgun.

It later transpired that the killers, being underage at the time they acquired the weapons, did so through an older fellow Columbine student and friend of Klebold, Robyn Anderson.

In exchange for her cooperation with the police investigation, no charges were brought against her, while two men were later convicted of supplying some of the weaponry and ammunition.

About a year before the killings, and with Harris having been required to attend anger management classes for a time after he and Klebold had been charged with trespass and theft – the charges later expunged in return for their participation in a rehabilitation programme – they had made a chilling video for a school project.

Entitled *Hitmen for Hire*, it featured the pair

raging at the camera and acting out the shooting and killing of students in the school hallway.

The massacre shocked America and sparked yet more debate on the highly controversial subject of gun control, while it also became the subject of the 2002 Michael Moore documentary *Bowling for Columbine*, winner of an Academy Award for Best Documentary Feature.

*Chapter four:*

# On the world stage

**With a reputation as a hell-raiser, Richard St John Harris was the award-winning Irish actor, film director, theatrical producer and singer better known as Richard Harris.**

Born in Limerick in 1930, the sixth of nine children, he was aged in his early twenties when he moved to England to pursue his chosen career as a theatrical director – but, unable to find any suitable training courses, he enrolled in the London Academy of Music and Dramatic Art to study acting.

Making his West End theatre debut in 1956 in a production of *The Quare Fellow*, his film debut came two years later in *Alive and Kicking*.

Other early film credits include the 1961 *The Guns of Navarone*, the 1962 *Mutiny on the Bounty*, the 1963 *This Sporting Life* – for which he won the Best Actor Award at the Cannes Film Festival and an Academy Award nomination – and, from 1967, *Camelot*.

Other major screen credits followed, notably the 1970 *A Man Called Horse* and, in the same year, *The Molly Maguires* and *Cromwell* while, as a singer, he enjoyed international chart success in 1968 with songwriter Jimmy Webb's *MacArthur Park*.

In the 1990s, his credits included the Western *Unforgiven*, starring with Clint Eastwood, and *Cry, the Beloved Country* while in 2000 he starred with Russell Crowe in *Gladiator*.

It was also in the early 2000s that he came to the attention of younger film audiences with his memorable role of Dumbledore in two of the *Harry Potter* series of films – the 2001 *Harry Potter and the Philosopher's Stone* and, completed shortly before his death in 2002, *Harry Potter and the Chamber of Secrets*.

Famed as an actor, Harris also acquired a degree of notoriety for his hell-raising lifestyle and heavy drinking during the 1960s and 1970s.

He was married and divorced twice, firstly to Elizabeth Rees-Williams, daughter of the politician David Rees-Williams, 1st Baron Ogmore, and the American actress Ann Turkel.

He was the father, through his first marriage, of the actors **Jamie** and **Jared Harris** and the film director **Damian Harris**.

Born in London in 1961, Jared Harris is known for television roles that include that of Lance Pryce in *Mad Men*, while his big screen credits include the 2002 *Mr Deeds* and, from 2012, *Lincoln*.

His brother Damian, born in 1958, has directing credits that include the 1989 *The Rachel Papers*.

Born in 1950 in Englewood, New Jersey, Edward Allen Harris is the American actor, director and screenwriter better known as **Ed Harris**.

Major screen credits the 1991 *The Truman Show*, the 1995 *Apollo 13* and the 2003 *The Hours* – all of which won him Academy Award nominations for Best Supporting Actor.

With other credits that include the 2001 *Enemy at the Gates* and the biopic *Nixon*, he is also known for his portrayal of American astronaut John Glenn in the 1983 *The Right Stuff*.

On British shores, **George Harris**, born in 1949, is the stage, radio, musical theatre, television and film actor noted for his role of Kingsley Shacklebolt in the *Harry Potter* series of films.

Also known for his role of Captain Simon Katanga in the 1981 *Raiders of the Lost Ark* and as a Somali warlord in the 2001 *Black Hawk Down*, his television credits include the medical drama *Casualty*.

Having had roles in both television and film since the tender age of nine, **Naomie Harris** is the British actress born in 1976.

With early television credits that include the remake of the science fiction series *The Tomorrow*

*People*, she is particularly noted for her role of Eve Monepenny – 'Miss Monepenny' – in the 2012 James Bond film *Skyfall*, while she is also set to reprise the role in the Bond movie *Spectre*, scheduled for release in the autumn of 2015.

Other credits include the 2002 *28 Days Later* and the second and third of the *Pirates of the Caribbean* series, while she also portrayed Winnie Mandela in the biopic *Mandela: Long Walk to Freedom*.

On American television screens, Harriet Sansom Harris, also sometimes credited as **Harriet Harris**, is the American actress best known for her roles of Bebe Glazier in the sitcom *Frasier* and as Felicia Tilman in the drama series *Desperate Housewives*.

Born in 1955 in Fort Worth, Texas, as a stage actress she won a Tony Award in 2002 as Featured Actress in a Musical for her role in *Thoroughly Modern Millie*, while film credits include the 1993 *Addams Family Values*.

Born in 1914 in The Bronx, New York City, Jonathan Charasuchin was the American character actor better known as **Jonathan Harris**.

With his lovable puppets Orville the Duck and Cuddles the Monkey, **Keith Harris** was the English ventriloquist born in 1947 in Lyndhurst, Hampshire and who died in 2015.

A popular act on a number of variety shows and host from 1982 to 1990 of his own television show, he had British chart success in 1982 with his single *Orville's Song*.

With screenwriting credits – some in collaboration with Michael Dougherty and Bryan Singer – that include the 2006 *Superman Returns* and the 2006 *X-Men: Apocalypse*, **Dan Harris** is the American writer and director born in 1979.

Director of the 2004 *Imaginary Heroes*, starring Sigourney Weaver and which was recognised for 'excellence in filmmaking' by the National Board of Review, along with Dougherty he also wrote the screenplay for the 2005 *Urban Legends: Bloody Mary*.

Both a film editor and director, **Jon Harris**, born in Sheffield in 1967, has major editing credits that include the 2000 *Snatch* and the 2010 *127 Hours*, for which he won a BAFTA Award – while other credits include the 2012 *The Woman in Black* and, from 2013, *Trance*.

Bearers of the Harris name have also excelled in the highly competitive world of sport.

Born in 1945 in the Pontypool suburb of Torfaen, South Wales, **John Harris** battled against the odds to establish himself as a champion Paralympian athlete.

Involved as a youth in not only gymnastics but also in rugby union and boxing, tragedy struck when aged 18 he was left with paralysis in his legs after falling from a big wheel in a holiday camp.

It was after a friend encouraged him to attend a gym to improve his fitness and give him a positive focus that he later joined a paraplegic sports club.

Selected for the British team for the discus, shot-put and light-heavyweight weightlifts events for the 1980 Paralympics, it was at the games four years later that he became world record holder in the discus, while at the 1988 games he won silver in the discus and bronze in the pentathlon.

Also having competed four years later in the pentathlon, 4x400-metres relay and javelin events and in 1996 in the pentathlon, he was inducted into the Welsh Sports Hall of Fame in 2013.

On the fields of European football, **Ron Harris**, nicknamed "Chopper" because of his reputation as a particularly tough defender, is the English former player born in 1944 in Hackney, London.

A leading player for Chelsea in the 1960s and 1970s, his autobiography is entitled *Chopper: A Chelsea Legend*, while in 2011 he was the recipient of a Special Recognition Award from the club.

He is the brother of the full-back **Allan Harris**,

born in 1942, and who also played for Chelsea in addition to other clubs including Coventry and Queen's Park Rangers.

From sport to music, **Jack Harris**, born in 1951 and a cousin of the footballing Harris brothers, is the English vocalist who enjoyed chart success with the progressive rock band The Alan Parson's Project.

On American shores, **Emmylou Harris** is the American singer and songwriter who, at the time of writing, is the recipient of thirteen Grammy Awards.

Born in Birmingham, Alabama in 1947, these include Best Americana Award for her album *Old Yellow Moon* and the 2005 Best Female Country Vocal Performance Award for *The Connection*.

Her 1987 collaboration with Linda Ronstadt and Dolly Parton resulted in the best-selling album *Trio* – that produced best-selling singles that include *To Know Him is To Love Him*.

Not only an English singer but also an actress, **Anita Harris**, born in 1942, had chart success with songs that include the 1964 *Lies*, the 1967 *Just Loving You* and, from 1968, her version of *The Anniversary Waltz*.

Best known as having been the presenter from 1971 until 1978 of the BBC television rock music show *The Old Grey Whistle Test*, **Bob Harris** – more affectionately known as "Whispering Bob Harris" – was born in Northampton in 1946.

An original presenter of the BBC Radio 6 digital music station, launched in 2002, he was awarded an OBE in 2011 for services to music broadcasting.

From music to art, **Anne Harris** is the acclaimed sculptor whose work has been exhibited throughout her native Canada, the United States, Europe and Asia.

Born in 1928 in Woodstock, Ontario, two of her works grace the official residence of the Canadian Prime Minister in Ottawa.

A number of best-selling authors also bear the proud name of Harris.

A former journalist and BBC television reporter, **John Harris** was born in 1957.

Although the author of non-fiction works that include his 1983 *Gotcha, the Media, the Government and the Falklands Crisis*, and the 1986 *Selling Hitler*, he is now best known for his historical fiction.

These include his first novel, the 1992 *Fatherland*, the 2006 *Imperium* and, from 2013, *An Officer and a Spy*.

Born in 1961 in Belfast, Northern Ireland, **Jane Harris** is the critically acclaimed novelist and writer of screenplays whose works include her 2006 *The Observations* and, from 2011, *Gillespie and I*.

Author of the 1999 novel *Chocolat*, winner of a number of awards that include the Creative Freedom Award and which was also successfully adapted for film starring Johnny Depp and Juliette Binoche, **Joanne Harris** was born in 1964 in Barnsley, Yorkshire.

The recipient of an MBE, her other top-selling novels include *The Lollipop Shoes*, *Peaches for Monsieur le Curé* and the *Rune* series of fantasy works based on Norse mythology.

In the genre known as urban fantasy, **Charlaine Harris**, born in 1951 in Tunica, Mississippi, is the American author noted for *The Southern Vampire Mysteries* series, also known as *The Sookie Stackhouse Novels* – adapted for the highly popular television series *True Blood* and with Anna Paquin in the role of Sookie.